Cover Design by Barry Littmann and Laurie Duren

Library of Congress Cataloging-in-Publication Data
Burstein, John.
    The cycle of life / Slim Goodbody ; illustrated by Terry Boles.
      p.   cm -- (Wonderful you)
    Summary: Describes the changes that take place as a human grows from egg to old age and compares the developments that occur in different animals.
    ISBN 1-57749-050-9 (alk. paper)
    1. Life cycle, Human--Juvenile literature. 2. Life cycles (Biology)--Juvenile literature. [1. Life cycle, Human. 2. Animal life cycles. 3. Growth.] I. Boles, Terry, ill.
II. Title. III. Series: Wonderful you (Minneapolis, Minn.)
QP83.8.B87   1997
571.8'1--dc21
                                                      97-17652
                                                        CIP
                                                        AC

Printed in Korea
First Printing, September 1997

01 00 99 98 97   7 6 5 4 3 2 1

Published by Fairview Press, 2450 Riverside Avenue South, Minneapolis, MN 55454.

For a current catalog of Fairview Press titles, call 1-800-544-8207. Publisher's Note: Fairview Press publishes books and other materials related to the subjects of family and social issues. Its publications, including *The Cycle of Life,* do not necessarily reflect the philosophy of Fairview Health System or its treatment programs.

The paper used in this publication meets the minimum requirements of American National Standard for Information Sciences—Permanence of Paper for Printed Library Materials, ANSI Z329.48-1984.

THE CYCLE OF LIFE

SLIM GOODBODY

illustrated by Terry Boles

Fairview Press
Minneapolis

Dedication

To my mother, who brought me into the world;
my wonderful son, who continues the cycle;
and my wife, who enriches my life with love.

THE CYCLE OF LIFE

The Cycle of Life is a story of change, and all living things play a role in this great adventure.

From the tiny ant
To the giant whale,
We're all a part of
This exciting tale.

Tadpoles grow up into frogs;
Piglets fatten into hogs;
Acorns sprout up into oaks;
Babies become older folks.

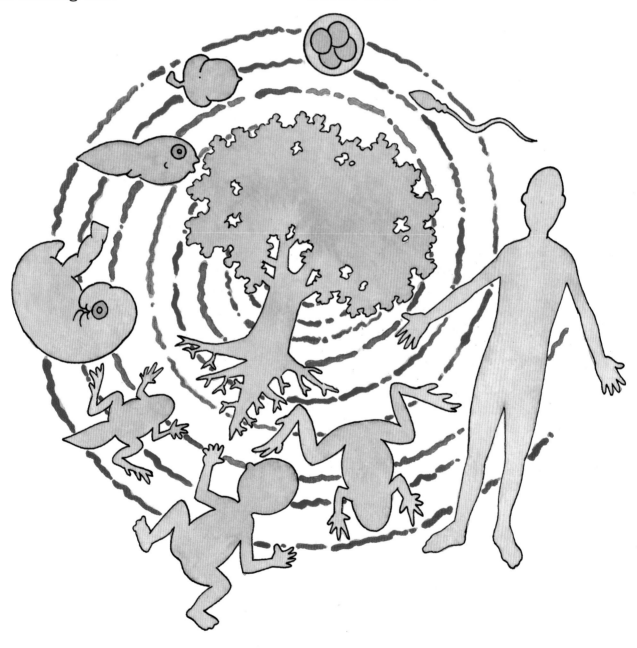

5

AGES AND STAGES

As every single creature ages,
It will pass through different stages.

From the moment you're born, you
start developing, changing, and growing
older. It's a process that happens gradually,
day by day, throughout your whole lifetime.

Though all of us age, no two people do it in exactly the same way at exactly the same time. We each have a kind of inner clock that controls the speed of our development, and when the time is right, we move to the next stage. That's why some babies crawl sooner than others, some children grow taller than others, some grown-ups get gray hair sooner than others, and so on.

But we are all moving in the same direction, carried along by the flow of time in the great adventure of life.

6

BEGINNINGS

Robins hatch from small blue eggs.
From seeds, red roses bloom.
And from an egg, you grew as well
Inside your mother's womb.

The first stage of your life's journey begins before you are born. You develop from a tiny egg inside your mother. This egg, which is much smaller than the head of a pin, joins with a sperm cell from your father, and you start to grow.

Inside your mother, the tiny egg comes to rest in a comfy, warm, and secure place called the womb. There you are given food and oxygen that flows through a special tube called the umbilical cord.

Amazing Facts

✳ You develop from an egg that is only 1/175 of an inch in diameter! That's much smaller than the period at the end of this sentence. You don't need a big egg to store your food because you receive nutrients directly from your mother.

✳ During your first 8 weeks in the womb, you're called an "embryo." An animal developing inside an egg and a plant developing inside a seed both have the same name.

✳ As a very young human embryo, you had tiny slits on your neck that looked something like the gills of a fish. You also had a tail! Both disappeared as you grew.

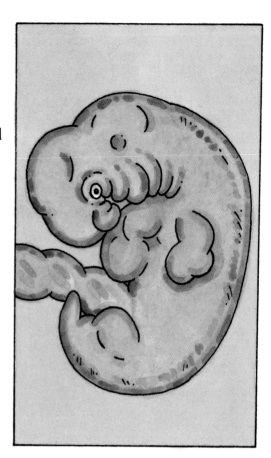

Life Around Us

Most creatures begin their lives inside some kind of egg. In birds, the egg leaves the mother's body and is protected by a hard shell. Otherwise the mother bird would be too heavy to fly! All the food the developing baby needs is inside the egg, contained within the yellow yolk.

Flowers come from eggs, too, Tiny eggs are hidden deep in a plant's flowers. When bees bring pollen, the eggs and pollen join to make seeds. The seeds fall to the ground and start to grow. The outer seed coat protects the little seedling and also contains stored food.

Many reptile mothers never get a chance to see their babies. A mama turtle will dig a hole in the sand or mud, lay her eggs inside, cover them up, and go away for good. But she still gives her babies a good start because they stay hidden from danger, and the sun provides the warmth they need to grow.

8

A mother cod fish will lay as many as 4 million eggs! These fish eggs are small and delicate like balls of jelly, with no shells to protect them. They are easily gobbled up by other fish, or if they're washed ashore, they soon dry up and die. Only a few eggs out of every million ever become baby fish.

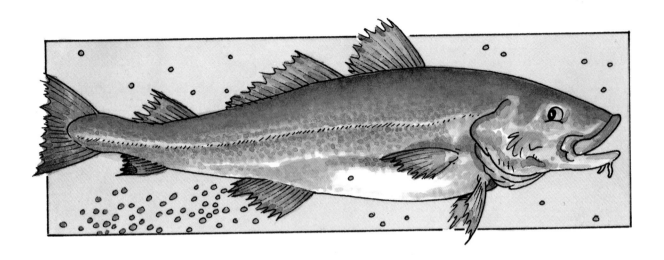

Think About

✳ Plants and animals may look very different, but they all have some things in common. For example, they all start small and grow bigger. Can you think of any other qualities they share?

BECOMING

In your cozy hideaway
You grow bigger day by day.
There your little beating heart
And other organs get their start.

Nine months pass, and when
    they're gone,
You are ready to move on.
Fully formed, from head to feet,
A little person, now complete.

Inside your mother's womb, you grow at an amazing rate—developing from a single egg into a baby made of trillions of cells in a few short months. Now you're big enough and strong enough to come out and greet the world.

Amazing Facts

✳ After you've grown inside your mother for 3 weeks, you're 1/10th of an inch long and your brain and spinal column begin to form.

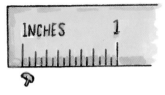

3 Weeks

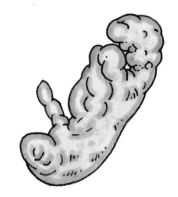

6 Weeks

✳ After 5 weeks or so, your heart starts beating, and by 6 weeks, your eyes, ears, and limbs are beginning to appear.

✳ From 9 weeks until birth, you're no longer an "embryo." You're now called a "fetus."

✳ At about 12 weeks, you're making your first small movements.

✳ The fastest growing period is the fourth month—you actually double in length. All your inner organs have formed by now.

✳ By 6 months you can open and close your eyes, and fingerprints are starting to appear.

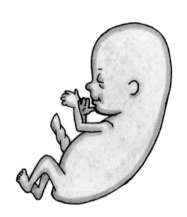

12 Weeks

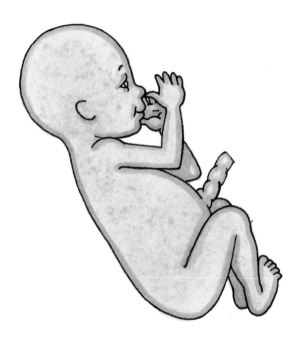

9 Months

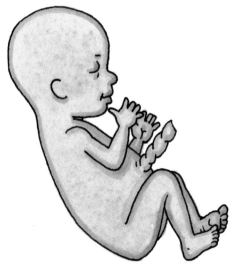

6 Months

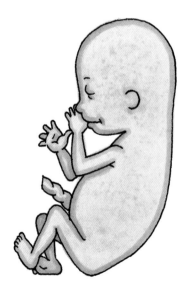

4 Months

✱ Some babies are born much earlier than expected, sometimes by as much as 8 or 9 weeks. They need extra help to survive. If they weigh under 5-1/2 pounds, they're called premature.

✱ An average baby weighs about 7 pounds. The largest baby ever on record weighed 23-3/4 pounds.

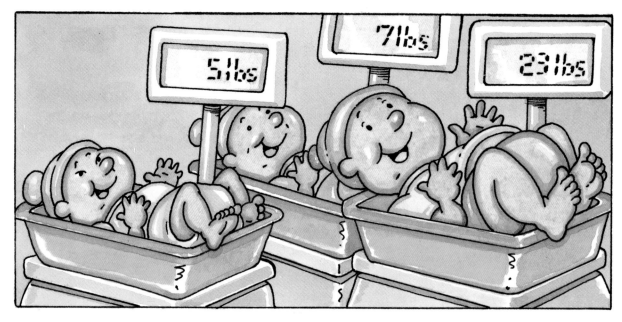

Think About

✱ Even though you spent 9 months inside your mother's womb, you can't remember the experience at all. Why do you think that is? Imagine how it may have felt to spend time there.

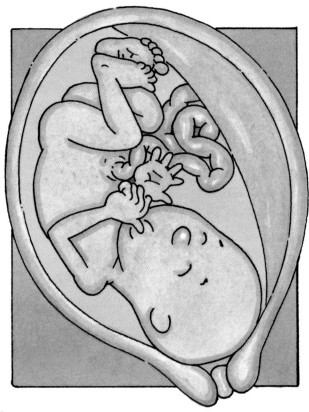

12

Life Around Us

A house mouse takes only 20 days to be born, kittens and puppies take 9 weeks, but an elephant takes 2 whole years!

Robins take 14 days to hatch from eggs, chicks take 21, and ducklings take 28.

The giant sequoia tree in California starts as a seed weighing much less than an ounce. It may end up growing 270 feet tall, with a trunk measuring 40 feet around and a weight over 12 million pounds!

HELLO, WORLD!

Full of promise, you are born,
Like the sunrise in the morn.
A world of light you will behold
When you're only seconds old.

You leave your cozy, warm home of 9 months and enter a world that's colder and a whole lot brighter. You take a breath of air—the very first breath you've ever taken on your own—and let out a cry: "WAAAA!"

The umbilical cord that connected you to your mother is cut. You don't need it anymore because you are a separate individual.

Amazing Facts

✳ Your belly button is the place where your umbilical cord used to be attached.

✳ After you're born, your kidneys and liver still need a little time to start working properly. It only takes a short while to get up to speed. Your circulation and blood need to adapt and change, too. This takes about 2 weeks.

Think About

✳ Inside the womb, you were attached to your mother by an umbilical cord. When you were born, you became a separate and unique individual. Your parents may be there to help and guide you, but your life is now your own. What are some of the things you'd like to do in life? Will they all include your family?

Life Around Us

When it is born, a baby porpoise is already half its mother's length.

The blue whale starts out as an egg weighing only a fraction of an ounce, but by the time it's born it weighs 2 or 3 tons!

A kangaroo gives birth to a baby that is only 3/4 of an inch long (about the size of a peanut). The only developed parts are the baby's front legs, which it uses to crawl into its mother's pouch. This pouch is warm and fur-lined, and contains a milk nipple for the baby to suck on. The baby won't leave the pouch for 10 to 12 months.

BUNDLE OF JOY

Newborn wonder,
Cuddly, cute,
Dressed up in
Your birthday suit.

Tiny infant
You arrive,
Needing help
To stay alive.

Fragile, helpless,
Soft and small,
Can't care for
Yourself at all.

But when you're in
A hungry mood,
You sure can cry
And wail for food.

But mostly you
Don't make a peep,
Because you're lying
Fast asleep.

Even though you're now a separate person, you're still absolutely helpless after you are born. You can't control your muscles, your vision is blurry, and you sleep most of the time. But your parents think you're a wonderful sight to behold.

Welcome to the world!

Amazing Facts

✳ Once you're born, you're no longer a fetus—you're called an infant.

✳ At first, newborns don't have the ability to sweat when they're hot or shiver when they're cold.

* Some babies are born with a full head of hair, as well as fine down on their ears, lower back, and shoulders.

* Some babies are born with teeth.

* During their first few weeks, babies sleep an average of 16 to 17 hours a day, and they're usually not awake for more than 2 hours at a time.

* A baby's heart is only 1/16th the size of a grown-up's heart, but it contains the same number of cells.

Think About

* Do babies sleep so much because they need to store energy? What would they use this energy for?

* Newborns are usually placed in a nursery for the first few days. People grow flowers in a nursery, too. Why do you think we use the same word?

* Parents sometimes call a baby "their bundle of joy." What do you suppose that means?

Life Around Us

A fawn can run and jump within an hour of being born, and a pronghorn antelope can run 25 miles an hour when it is only a day old.

Newborn puppies and kittens are blind and helpless.

The largest animal to give birth to a helpless youngster is the bear. Mom might weigh several hundred pounds, and the bear cub may weigh only a few ounces.

Baby whales and dolphins are the most active of all newborns. They start swimming alongside their mothers from the moment of birth!

Giraffe and zebra babies can stand up and walk within minutes of being born.

Like human babies, animal babies cry to express their needs, but they use different sounds than human babies do. Rhino calves squeal, chickadees cheep, puppies whimper, kittens mew, and hamsters squeak.

FIRST TIMES

First you crawl,
Then you walk.
First you babble,
Then you talk.
So many firsts along the way,
Heading toward your first birthday

You don't remain a helpless newborn
for long, and your first year is full of
adventure. From the moment you're
born, you start learning. Your ability to
move, understand, and let others know
what you want improves day by day.
With help, you take your first steps.
There's a whole world waiting for you
and you're ready to get into the action!

Amazing Facts

✳ You gain control of your body from the top down: first your head and neck, next your arms and trunk, and finally your legs.

✳ Some babies don't crawl; they sit until they learn to stand up.

✳ Some babies learn to stand, but don't know how to sit back down. They will stand for hours until someone helps them sit. But they soon learn how to do it themselves.

✳ Your bones, which were very soft when you were born, are starting to get harder.

Life Around Us

Until you can walk, you are carried or pushed in a stroller when you go out with mom or dad. Baby animals also depend on their parents:

Kangaroo babies ride along in pouches.
Monkey babies hold on to a parent's back.
Nile crocodile babies ride around in their mama's teeth!

A mama sea otter plays with her pups by tossing them into the air and catching them. When she dives for food, she leaves them hidden in a bed of kelp.

Think About

* During your first year there are many things you'll do for the first time. Here's just a few. Can you think of any others?

First breath   First smile
First laugh   First word
First hug   First step

* You're blessed because you belong to a family. Since one of the ways you learn best is by imitating, who do you think your first teachers are?

ON THE MOVE

Another year and you're a toddler,
A super-active little waddler.

Every moment on the go,
Reaching high and touching low,
Now you're over, now you're under,
You're a tiny natural wonder.

As a toddler, you can get around by yourself—and once that happens, there's no stopping you! You're all over the place—under the sink, in the closet, behind the couch—a ball of energy! You're hungry for discovery, and the more you move, the more you're able to learn about your world.

Amazing Facts

✳ Most babies start walking when they're 12–15 months old, but some babies begin as early as 9 months or as late as 16 months.

✳ The word "toddler" comes from the first kind of walking you do, which is called toddling. It's a kind of flat-footed paddling along with your toes out to the side.

✳ Some babies would rather crawl, even when they know how to walk. That's because they can crawl faster!

✳ At 18 months, you're starting to run; by the age of 2, you're running easily.

✳ During your first 2-1/2 years, all 20 of your baby teeth will probably grow in.

✳ You grow faster during the first 2 years of your life than you ever will again.

Life Around Us

You communicate using words. By age two, you're able to put two-word sentences together, like "See house" or "Me hungry." Animals also communicate—to warn others, scare enemies, get help, or sometimes to invite another animal over for company. Here's how:

Geese honk

Whales sing

Otters whistle

Wolves howl

Horses whinny

Owls hoot

Foxes yap

Chickens cluck

Chipmunks chatter

Think About

✳ As a toddler, you start saying "NO!" to things. Sometimes that can be frustrating to others. But if you never said no, and never developed ideas and a will of your own, wouldn't that make you a kind of living robot? How is learning to choose for yourself an important part of becoming your own person? How can you can develop your will in positive YES ways?

THE GREAT DETECTIVE

They say a kitten's curious;
That certainly is true.
But kitties never show more
Curiosity than you!

You're an eager young detective
Who loves to poke and pry.
You've got a ton of questions,
And you're always asking why!

You've become a bold, daring, and incredibly curious preschooler, who's always getting into everything. You have a terrific imagination and you love to play. Believe it or not, playing is one of the most important ways you learn. It teaches you how to think, plan, use your muscles skillfully, and get along with others.

You're making new friends and learning to take turns. Instead of grabbing, hitting, or crying, you're using words to ask for what you want. Every day you're growing in mind, body, and spirit.

Amazing Facts

* By the time you're 4 years old:

    you have the muscle coordination and balance of an adult.

    all your baby teeth have grown in.

    you need 10–12 hours of sleep a night to stay healthy.

    you know about 1,500 words and will learn about 1,000 more before your fifth birthday.

* At age 4 or 5, boys and girls are equally strong.

Think About

✳ Preschoolers love to ask questions about the meaning of everything they see, hear, or think about. Here are just a few. Can you think of any others? How does asking questions help you learn?

What is it?

How come?

How soon do we get there?

Where is it?

Why do I have to?

Why does the sun shine?

Why can't the cat talk?

Why is the sky blue?

Why is the grass green?

Why do dogs have tails?

✳ The ages of 3 and 4 are sometimes called the "magic years" because you use your imagination so much. Do you like playing games of make-believe? Why?

Life Around Us

Playing is an important part of learning for animals, too.

Young chimpanzees like to play tag. They chase each other in and out among the trees, which makes them better climbers when they grow up.

Fighting games between brother and sister lion and tiger cubs helps them learn how to attack and defend themselves—skills they'll need later in life.

Seal pups snort and play tag in the water, helping them become better swimmers.

When animals pretend, they are protecting themselves, not just having fun.

Frilled lizards are small and helpless, but they pretend to be big and dangerous. When they open their mouths, their throats are bright red and frightening and a flap of skin on their neck lifts up and folds out. They look big and scary!

Harmless hog-nosed snakes open their mouths and hiss, pretending they're going to bite. If the enemy isn't frightened, they roll over, lie still, and pretend to be dead.

SCHOOL DAYS

The years roll by
And now you're five.
Wow, it's great
To be alive.
In the years
Since your debut,
Look at all
You've learned to do!

You can
Dress yourself,
Tie your shoe,
Brush your teeth,
Play kazoo,
Use a crayon,
Cut and glue,
Hop just like
A kangaroo,
And help someone
Who's only two!

You're ready to begin the next big adventure of your life: going to school. You learn all kinds of things—not only about reading and writing, but also about yourself. You learn lessons that help prepare you for taking charge of your life when you become a grown-up. You also start looking up to older kids and trying to act like them. You still love your family very much, but you're realizing that they're not the only people in the world who are important.

Amazing Facts

✳ It's important to remember that we all have our own kind of inner clock, so we all learn and develop at different rates. That means that some children learn things faster or slower than others.

✳ Wolfgang Amadeus Mozart, one of the world's greatest composers, was touring the courts of Europe, playing music for kings and queens, when he was only 5. He was also composing music!

✳ Albert Einstein, one of the greatest scientists who ever lived, took so long in learning to talk, his parents were worried that he wasn't very smart. But when he was ready, he changed the world!

Life Around Us

We learn by going to school, but animals learn from their parents:

> Seals learn to swim by riding on their mother's back.

> Baby bears learn what to eat by following mama around and eating what she does.

You love to run fast—but how about some of these animal speedsters:

> A dragonfly can fly 35 miles per hour (mph).

> A tuna can swim 65 mph.

> A cheetah can run 71 mph.

> A duck hawk can fly 175 mph.

> A peregrine falcon can dive 224 mph.

Think About

✳ As you get older, you learn to take more responsibility for yourself. You're discovering that your actions have consequences. For example, if you don't put things away, you may not find them the next day. These kind of lessons prepare you for taking charge of your life when you grow up. Can you think of any other examples?

CRUISING ALONG

The next few years, your body's
  growing,
But the rate of speed is slowing.
It's almost like you need to take
A well-deserved and welcome
  break.

You've been growing and
changing at a lightning-fast clip.
But between ages 6 and 9,
things will slow down and you
can cruise along for a bit. Your
growth hasn't stopped—your
body and mind are still developing—but the rate has become
more gradual and steady.

Enjoy the pace, because soon you'll be off and running again!

Amazing Facts

❋ Between the ages of 6 and 9:

your permanent teeth begin to grow in.
(This starts earlier in girls.)

you'll spend more than 4,000 hours in
school.

boys and girls are about equal in height.

❋ Your body's proportions are changing
and you have a more "grown-up" look.
When you were a baby, your head was
very big compared to the rest of your
body, but now your head is growing more
slowly, and your legs are growing more
quickly. Even so, your head will reach its
full size before your feet do.

Think About

* As you get older, you become more concerned about what other kids say and do. You may want to dress like they do, or have the same kind of haircut. Can you think of any other examples? Why do you think that this is happening?

* You are developing your own inner sense of what is right and wrong—your conscience. How could listening to your conscience be helpful? Do you listen to yours?

Life Around Us

By now, you've learned good table manners. You can use a knife, fork, and spoon. Birds do things a little differently:

A parrot uses its bill as a nutcracker to open nuts and seeds.

A sparrow uses its bill like a tweezer to pick up small things on the ground.

A woodpecker drills a hole in a tree's bark with its bill to get to insects.

A heron uses its sharp bill to spear passing fish.

TEEN TIME

Your book of life
Turns a page.
Now you've reached
A brand new stage,
With double digits
In your age.

10, 11, 12 and then . . .
You're a teen-age citizen.

You're an adolescent now, and the changes you go through now are more remarkable than at any other time in your life, except for when you were growing inside your mother's womb. When you grew inside your mother, you developed the body of a baby. During adolescence, you'll develop the body of an adult.

Physical changes happen naturally, but growing up also calls for changes in how you act. That can be a bit harder, because you need to think about what's important to you, and decide how to make good choices. You have to learn to control yourself, and understand your feelings and the feelings of others.

Amazing Facts

✳ The changes in your body usually begin with a 2- or 3-year "growth spurt." Your internal clock controls when your growth spurt will begin and how fast you'll grow.

✳ Your feet start growing first, followed by your calves, thighs, hips, chest, and shoulders. The length of your trunk and the depth of your chest develop last of all.

✳ During adolescence, your heart becomes larger and stronger while your heart rate and breathing rate slow down.

✳ Girls usually begin their growth spurt at age 10-1/2. Boys usually begin it at 12-1/2. That means a 12- or 13-year-old girl is often taller and heavier than a boy her age.

✳ Boys soon catch up because they grow about 4 inches a year, while girls only grow about 3. Boys get about 45 pounds heavier, and girls gain 35 pounds during their teenage years.

✳ Your whole body is involved in growing—all your muscles, bones, and organs. Even your eyeballs expand from front to back. Your face changes, too: your chin gets pointier and your nose grows longer.

✳ Boys reach 98 percent of their adult height by age 17-1/2, and girls by age 16-1/2.

✳ The tallest person on record grew to be 8' 10-3/4". The shortest was only 16 inches tall.

Life Around Us

When human males grow up, they're usually bigger than human females, but that's not always the case with other species in nature. For example, a female deep-sea anglerfish is 3 feet long, and the male measures just 2-1/2 inches!

As your body gets bigger, your skin grows and stretches to fit. But that's not true for snakes and some lizards. They actually get too big for their skin and crawl right out of it. Of course, they've grown a new skin underneath that fits just fine.

31

Think About

* Adolescence is a time when you really begin to question yourself. You may start asking: What kind of person am I? Am I better (or worse) than others in some ways? What kind of person do I want to be? Why do I like some people and not others?

* During adolescence you become physically capable of having a baby. But that doesn't mean adolescents should have babies. Do you think young people who are still in school, still depending on their parents to take care of them, are ready to have babies of their own?

* By the time you reach your teenage years, all your permanent teeth have grown in, with the exception of the last 4 molars, which erupt at ages 17 and 21. These are called your "wisdom teeth." Why do you think they have that name?

32

ALL GROWN UP

You're in your twenties, fully grown.
Time to head out on your own,
Off to see what you can find,
Strong in body and in mind.

You're not a kid, your childhood's gone,
But in your heart, the child lives on

You've arrived at a special turning point, where adolescence ends and young adulthood begins. Though you're grown, you never leave your child self completely behind. Your early experiences have helped you become who you are as an adult.

Young adulthood is usually the healthiest time of life. You're grown up, independent, and at the peak of your physical abilities.

Amazing Facts

✳ Human beings have the longest childhood of any animal because most of our behavior is learned, not inherited. It takes time to gain the knowledge and skills you'll need as an adult.

✳ Your ears and nose will still grow (slowly), even when you've reached your full height.

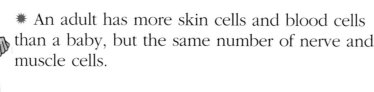

✳ An adult has more skin cells and blood cells than a baby, but the same number of nerve and muscle cells.

✳ You'll reach your peak of muscular strength when you're between 25 and 30 years old.

Think About

✳ You've learned many lessons from your childhood, but what you did then might not be such a good idea when you're older. For example, racing on a bike was fun, but racing in a car is dangerous. A lot of accidents happen to young adults at their physical peak. Do young adults tend to take more risks? If so, why?

✳ Do you think that the freedom you'll feel as a young adult (being independent and getting around on your own) is similar to the freedom you felt as a toddler learning to walk on your own two feet?

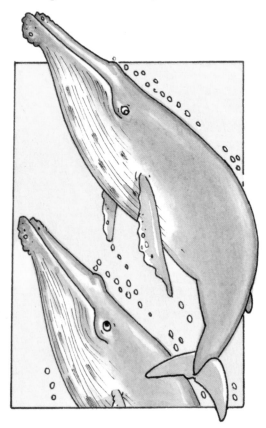

Life Around Us

A baby rat becomes an adult in 3 months, a fox grows up in a year, and a bear leaves home when it's 3.

Many animals stop growing at a certain age, but whales and elephants get bigger their whole lives.

Plants also grow throughout their lives. The tallest tree ever measured was a redwood that stood 364 feet tall!

34

YOUR TURN

Your great grandma
Had children who
Had children who
Had children, too.

The next in line
For kids, is you.
And the cycle of life
Flows right on through.

It's your turn to become a parent. You're old enough, wise enough, and responsible enough to have a baby of your own. Together with your partner you will love and cherish this new life. You'll learn to set a good example, to be a caring teacher and a thoughtful guide.

One day, your child will grow up and become a parent, too. This pattern exists throughout nature. No individual creature lives forever, so if a species is to survive, the gift of life must be passed from generation to generation.

Some people have no children and some have several. It's an individual choice that adults make for themselves. You'll choose to do whatever is right for you.

Amazing Facts

✳ 9 out of 10 adults get married.

✳ A Russian woman has the record for the most children—she had 69 kids, including 16 pairs of twins, 7 sets of triplets, and 4 sets of quadruplets.

✳ The oldest mother gave birth at age 63.

Life Around Us

Animals have different parenting arrangements:

With robins, blackbirds, and sparrows, the male and female work together building the nest, sitting on eggs, and feeding the young.

With deer, bear, rabbits, and hummingbirds, the male leaves, and the female raises her young alone.

With baboons, pheasants, and elks, one male has several mates. When the babies are born, he stays around to protect them.

Some female bugs lay 30–40 tiny eggs on a leaf, guard them for 3 weeks until they hatch, and then continue to protect them.

Most babies look like miniature versions of their parents, but some look totally different when they're born. For example, the caterpillar grows up to become a butterfly, and a tadpole develops into a frog.

Think About

✻ Have you ever seen a relay race? The runner circles the track and hands the baton off to the next in line. In what ways is this like having children? How is it different?

✻ Parents need to teach their children to respect themselves and have confidence in what they can do. When you grow up and become a parent, what are some of the things you might say to help your children learn to believe in themselves?

SLOWING DOWN

When gray hair appears
In your middle-age years,
It really can seem a bit strange.

Though you may exclaim,
"I still feel the same!"
Your body is starting to change.

New wrinkles begin
On your middle-aged skin.
You can't move as fast you did.

And while you may state,
"I'm still feeling great!"
You're clearly no longer a kid.

Middle age begins when you're about 35 years old and ends when you're about 65. During these years a lot is happening. You're raising a family, working hard, doing your share for your community, and enjoying your friendships. You might become a grandparent, too.

Since your twenties, you've been slowly and gradually losing certain abilities, but until now you haven't really noticed any differences. You still feel great, but some of these changes are starting to show. For example, even if you've never worn glasses before, now you might need them to read. You may do things a little more slowly, but your wisdom and experience allow you to be more accurate and efficient.

Now that you are midway on your life's journey, you're also examining your life in a new way. You think about your youthful goals and dreams, what you've done up to now, and what you still want to do.

Amazing Facts

✳ Almost half the United States population is now middle-aged.

✳ Changes happen gradually throughout your middle-age years, but by the time you're 55 years old or so, here's what's probably happened:

Your skin has thinned, which leads to sagging and wrinkling.

Your hair has thinned or turned gray because of loss of the body protein called melanin. Some people's hair turns gray when they are in their twenties.

You can't hear higher frequency sounds as well as you did before, so sometimes it's hard to identify voices.

The bones in your spine settle, and you're now about an inch shorter than you were when you were 18. (By the time you're 80, you'll "shrink" another inch or so.)

The muscles of your back and legs lose some strength. Your arm muscles retain most of their power.

The number of taste buds on your tongue has decreased, so you've lost some ability to taste food.

You'll need less sleep than you did when you were young.

Think About

✳ A 6-year-old thinks a 15-year-old is old.
A 20-year-old thinks a 40-year-old is old.
A 60-year-old thinks an 80-year-old is old.
What do you think it means to be old?
Does a newborn baby think you're old?

Life Around Us

Because animals have different life spans, they reach middle age in different years of their lives:

Robins reach middle age when they're 5.

Dogs reach middle age when they're 6.

Horses reach middle age when they're 12.

An Indian elephant reaches middle age at 35, the same age as humans do.

OLD-TIMER

When the years you've been alive
Finally number sixty-five,
You begin a brand new stage,
Growing into your old age.

Many years have passed, it's true,
But many lie ahead of you.
You're life has turned another page,
You're moving onward through old age.

You never cease to learn and grow;
The more you age, the more you know.
With all you've done, you're very wise,
Though you look old to other's eyes.

Old age can be a very special time of life. During your earlier years, you had the chance to learn, grow, have a family, and do meaningful work. All these opportunities have helped you become the incredible person you are now.

All the lessons you've learned and the experiences you've had are still within you, and each day you continue to gain wisdom and deeper understanding.

Growing old happens gradually, just like growing up. It's a process that can last 10, 20, 30, 40, or even 50 years. In many ways, life comes full circle. When you were born, people took care of you. Then you grew up and took care of yourself. When you had children, you took care of others. Now that you're old, you rely on others to help care for you again.

Think About

✳ In Greek mythology, there is a story about the hero Oedipus who was asked this riddle by the Sphinx: "What walks on 4 legs in the morning, 2 legs in the afternoon, and 3 legs in the evening?" Do you know the answer?

✳ There's a story in the Bible about a man named Methuselah, who lived 900 years! Would you like to live that long? What are some of the things you'd do with all your time?

✳ It's important to remember that no two people are the same, and that someone's age doesn't mean they have to act a certain way. For example, someone who is 80 might have the same interests as someone who is 30—like bowling or reading. Can you think of any things you like to do, that someone who is 80 would also enjoy?

Amazing Facts

✳ After age 60, most people lose some sensitivity to pain. It also takes longer for cuts and bruises to heal.

✳ A special branch of medicine, called geriatrics, treats people who are old. Gerontology is an area of science that studies normal aging.

✳ Both the very old and very young can't really tell how hot or cold something is.

✳ Between the ages of 20 and 90, the brain loses a little weight. There's some memory loss, but old people can still be bright and alert, and can think very clearly.

✳ Each year you're alive, your heart rate slows down by about one beat per minute.

Life Around Us

There's a sequoia tree named The General Sherman that's 3,800 years old.

A rat reaches old age when it's 2, an ostrich reaches old age at 58, and an Andean condor reaches old age at 65.

LIFE AND DEATH

There comes a time when all things die.
We don't know when, we're not sure why.
But life and death will always blend,
And what begins must also end.

Life isn't always measured in the number of years we've lived, but in what we've experienced in those years.

We're a part of the world we live in, and nature moves in cycles. Plants, animals, and people are born, they live, and then they die. If we all lived forever, there wouldn't be any room for new life.

We inherit the world from those who came before, and we leave it to those who will follow. We're given so much in life—a family, love, and a chance to grow and learn. In return, we all leave something—a child, a grandchild, a new idea, a job well done, or a memory that makes others feel warm inside. The important thing in life is to make a difference, to leave the world a better place than it was before we came into it.

Amazing Facts

✳ People today can expect to live for about 75 years. That's changed a lot from the way it was in the past:

For the ancient Greeks of 500 B.C., life expectancy was only 18 years.

For the Romans of 1000 A.D., the life expectancy was 25 years.

For United States citizens in 1900 A.D. (just a century ago), life expectancy was only 35.

✳ In the village of Abkhasia, Russia, there are reports of people who are 140 years old.

* People whose parents and grandparents lived longer lives than most others, tend to live longer, too.

* On average, women live longer than men.

Life Around Us

Animals have different life spans. Remember, these are only averages. Some will live longer and some shorter:

Robin	10 years	Dog	12 years
Monkey	15 years	Horse	25 years
Lion	29 years	Boa constrictor	40 years
Blue whale	45 years	Indian elephant	78 years

A mayfly lives its whole life in just a few days.

Plants have different life spans:

Zinnias, marigolds, corn, wheat, beans, and peas complete their entire life in one season.

Beets and carrots live for two years.

Lilies and daisies live for several years.

Sequoia and redwood trees live for hundreds of years.

Think About

* There is a Greek legend about a bird called the Phoenix. It was said that when it died, it was burned in a fire. A brand new bird came out of the ashes. Every time it aged and died, it was reborn. What do you think the Greeks are trying to tell us in this tale?

✳ If animals and plants lived forever, what do you think the world would be like? Do you think it would get too crowded?

✳ There's a saying that goes, "Where I am, death is not. Where death is, I am not." What do you think this means? If you are afraid of death, can this saying help? How?

THE CYCLE OF LIFE

The blossoms of a summer's day,
In the winter fade away.
But in spring the fertile ground
Once again is flower-crowned.

Endings lead to new beginnings,
Losses later lead to winnings,
And the cycle keeps on spinning,
Yes, the cycle keeps on spinning.

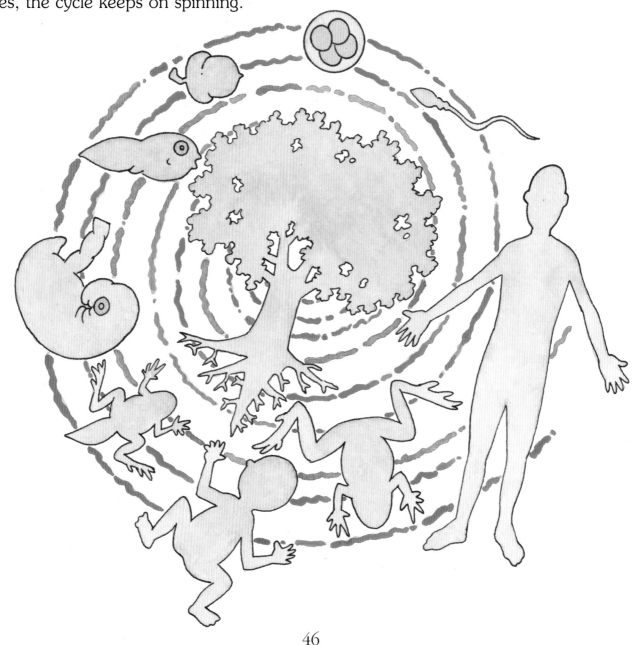